Renderings
Selected Translations

RENDERINGS
SELECTED TRANSLATIONS
by
William Baer

Measure Press
Savannah, Georgia

The text of this book is composed in Baskerville.
Composition by R.G.
Manufacturing by Ingram.

Baer, William
  Renderings: Selected Translations / by William Baer — 1st ed.

  ISBN-13: 978-1-939574-40-4
  ISBN-10: 1-939574-40-4
  Library of Congress Control Number: 2025944373

Measure Press
2 Longberry Lane
Savannah, GA 31419
http://www.measurepress.com/measure/

Acknowledgements:

The author wishes to thank the editors of the publications in which some of these translations originally appeared:

Able Muse, Acumen, Atlanta Review, First Things, London Magazine, Modern Age, Modern Poetry in Translation, National Review, The New Criterion, New Letters, Poetry Salzburg Review, Portuguese Literary and Cultural Studies, Presence, Saint Ann's Review, and *The Wanderer.*

Some of these translations also appeared in:

"Borges" and Other Sonnets, Truman State University Press, 2003.
Luís de Camões: Selected Sonnets, University of Chicago Press, 2005.
"Bocage" and Other Sonnets, Texas Review Press, 2008.
Formal Salutations: New & Selected Poems, Measure Press, 2019.

For my family and friends
— especially Willis

CONTENTS

"There's another rendering now; but still one text."

— *Moby-Dick*

Catullus

Carmen CI

I've come across the nations and the seas,
beloved brother, to stand upon your grave,
to bring to you, at last, these gifts for the dead,
speaking softly, in vain, to your silent ashes.
The Fates have taken you away from me,
too soon, too premature, too unexpected.
Nevertheless, please accept these gifts,
in the tradition of our beloved forefathers,
as my tears rise again in my eyes and swell:
Goodbye, brother, forever! Hail and farewell!

Gāius Valerius Catullus
(Roman, c.84–c.54 B.C.E.)

Catullus

Carmen VII

You ask, my Lesbia, how many kisses
are enough, more than enough, for me?
As many as the Libyan grains of sand
lying in Silphium-blooming Cyrene
between the oracle of sultry Jove
and the sacred tomb of old King Battus;
Or as many stars that in the silent night
spy upon the secret loves of lovers.
To kiss you with so many kisses would be
enough, more than enough, for crazed Catullus,
which all the prying eyes could never count,
nor evil tongues bewitch.

Gāius Valerius Catullus
(Roman, c.84–c.54 B.C.E.)

Catullus

Carmen CII

If ever a secret was entrusted to someone
whose loyalty of spirit was clearly known,
you'll find that I am also loyalty-bound
and think that I've become Harpocrates.*

* the Roman god of silence and secrets

Gāius Valerius Catullus
(Roman, c.84–c.54 B.C.E.)

Vergil

The Death of Dido

Aeneid, *from Book IV*

"Great Sun, surveyor of all the works of the earth,
Juno, who apprehends my miseries,
Hecate, bewailed at night throughout the cities,
and you, avenging Furies, and all the gods,
listen to dying Dido, listen to my cries,
and use your sacred powers to answer my prayers!
If accursed Aeneus should reach that harbor
and sail to land, as Jupiter decrees,
so be it, but let him be harassed in war
by a fearless people willing to fight,
let him be torn from the arms of his young son,
let him beg for help and watch his soldiers die,
and when he surrenders to a vindictive peace,
may he never enjoy the life he's hoping for,
but, instead, let him die before his time
and lie unburied on the barren sand!
I pray for this, poured out with my last blood.
And you, my loyal subjects, pursue with hatred
the prince's kin and all his coming descendants
then offer it all in tribute to my ashes!
Allow no peace or treaties between our peoples,
and let some great Avenger rise from my blood,
hunt down the Trojans with swords and flaming torches,
either now or in days to come, coast against coast,
wave against wave, arms against arms, forever!"

When done, she turned her thoughts in another direction,
considering how to destroy her hateful life.
Briefly, she spoke to Barce, Sychaeus's nurse
(since Dido's nurse was dead in her native land):
"Dear nurse, please bring my sister Anna here,
and tell her to hurry and sprinkle herself with water
and bring the sacrificial offerings.
Then you must bind your hair with holy fillets.
I plan to finish the rites of Stygian Jupiter,
which I've already prepared, and put an end
to the sorrows and pains of my unrequited love
and set the pyre of the Trojan prince on fire."

Quickly, the elderly nurse left her queen,
as Dido, wild with desperate intentions,
rolled her bloodshot eyes, as her trembling cheeks
flecked with bright red flashes, even though
she was mostly pale at the thought of approaching death.
Frantically, she burst through the inner doorway
and climbed the funeral pyre and drew the sword
that once was a treasured gift from the Trojan prince.
But then, she noticed the prince's abandoned clothes
and the bed they knew so well. She paused a moment,
wept with memories, then flung herself down on the bed:
"O Remnants so sweet, back when the gods approved,
accept my spirit and release me from my sorrows.
I've lived my life, living what the Fates allowed,
and now my spirit will pass to the Underworld.
I've built a famous city and seen its battlements.
I've avenged my husband. I've punished a hostile brother.
And I was happy, alas, too happy! If only
the Trojan ships had never come to shore!"

Then she pressed her face into her bed and cried:
"I die unavenged! But let me die anyway
since it pleases me to descend into the darkness.
Let Aeneus watch the pyre's fire from his ship
and take with him the omen of my death!"

Then Dido's servants saw her falling on her sword
which foamed with blood, which drenched her bloody hands.
Their piercing screams rose high above the courtyard
and rumors ran riot throughout the horrified city.
The roofs resounded with pitiful lamentations,
and the heavens echoed the city's terrible cries,
as if great Carthage or ancient Tyre had fallen
to a conquering enemy, as the raging flames
rolled over the roofs of men and gods.

Publius Vergilius Maro
(Roman, 70–19 B.C.E.)

Horace

Ode I.11

Don't ask, Leuconoe, what we're forbidden to know:
how much time the gods have given to you and me.
Don't bother with Babylonian fortune tellers,
it's best to endure whatever is meant to be,
whether Jupiter will grant us other winters,
or whether the current winter will be our last,
which stirs the Tyrrhenian sea against the rocks.
Be sensible, strain your wine, don't look ahead,
for as we speak envious time has flown.
Refrain from trusting the future, seize the day!

> Quintus Horatius Flaccus
> (Roman, 65–8 B.C.E.)

Martial

Epigram V.9

When I was tired, you came immediately,
accompanied by a hundred of your students,
whose hundred freezing hands then checked my pulse.
I had no fever then, but *now* I do!

Marcus Valerius Martialis
(Roman, c.40–c.104 C.E.)

Martial

Epigram X.61

Here lies Erotion, hastened to her grave
by unkind Fates during her sixth winter.
May whoever owns these lands in the future
continue to place flowers on her grave each year.
And may the gods keep your children safe,
and may this stone remain the only tragic one.

> Marcus Valerius Martialis
> (Roman, c.40–c.104 C.E.)

Anonymous

The Death of Roland

La Chanson de Roland, laisse 176

After the Ambush at Roncevaux Pass:

Count Roland lies beneath a pine
and turns his face to Spain.
He recollects so many things:
the lands that he'd once conquered,
his noble kin, his home sweet France,
and Charlemagne who'd raised him.
These memories make him weep and sigh,
but he doesn't neglect his soul.
He confesses his sins and asks forgiveness:
"My Father, who knows no falsehood,
who saved dead Lazarus from the grave,
and Daniel from the lions,
protect my soul from every peril,
from the sins I have committed."
He offers his right-hand glove to God
and the angel Gabriel takes it.
He rests his head down on his arms
and clasps his hands and dies.
Then God sends down a Cherubin angel,
with Michael of the Perils,
he also sends down the angel Gabriel,
and they bear his soul to heaven.

Anonymous
(French, c.1040–1115 C.E.)

Anonymous

The Rescue of Doña Elvira and Doña Sol

El Cantar de mio Cid, from laisse 131

[*At the suggestion of Don Alfonso, King of Castile, the warrior Cid allows his two young daughters, Elvira and Sol, to marry the Carrión heirs, Diego and Fernando González. The brothers prove to be both cowards and traitors and after collecting their undeserved share of booty from the Cid's military victories, they decide to leave Valencia, return to Carrión, and murder their wives. During the journey back to Carrión, they strip and viciously beat Elvira and Sol, leaving them for dead. Fortunately, Félix Muñoz, the Cid's loyal cousin, searches for his missing two cousins.*]

When the *Carrión*s rode by   spurring their horses,
Félix Muñoz   retraced their tracks,
finding his cousins,   who lay half-dead.
"Cousins, Cousins!"   He jumped from his mount,
tethered his horse,   and rushed to their side:
"Doña Elvira!   Doña Sol!
Look at the evils   your husbands have done!
May God and Mary   let justice be done!"
He turned them over,   the cousins he loved,
who seemed so lifeless   unable to speak.
It seemed as though   his heart would break:
"Cousins, Cousins!   Elvira and Sol!
For the love of God,   wake up, my cousins,

the sun still shines,   but night is coming,
when ravenous beasts   will surely attack!"
Then Sol and Elvira   began to revive;
they opened their eyes   and heard their cousin:
"For the love of God,   be brave, my cousins,
for when your husbands   learn that I'm gone,
they'll come back fast   and hunt us down,
and we'll die right here   unless God helps."
Then Doña Sol   spoke out in pain:
"To honor our father,   the warrior Cid,
give us some water   in the name of God!"
So Félix Muñoz   filled up his hat,
which was clean and new   and came from Valencia,
and he offered his cousins   water to drink,
who despite their condition   drank it right down.
Insistent, but gentle,   he encouraged his cousins
to sit themselves up   and they did as he asked.
Then urging them on   he helped them to stand
and lifted them both   onto his horse,
covering their nakedness   with his cloak.
He took the reins   and led them quickly,
completely alone,   through Corpes Forest
to finally emerge   beyond the mountains,
to make his way   to the Duero River
and safety at the tower   of Doña Urraca . . .

Anonymous
(Spanish, c.1140–1207 C.E.)

Dante

Paolo and Francesca

Inferno, *from Canto V*

"Could I speak to those two lovers who've sinned,
together, in betrayal and lust, and now appear
to whirl forever, endless, upon the wind?"

"Be ready," Vergil advised, "when they come near,
and call to them as they come whirling through,
and maybe they'll find a way to visit us here."

So when the whirlwinds brought them back in view,
I called out loud, "Lovers, would it be all right,
within your torment, if I could speak with you?"

Immediately, they rose within the hellish night,
like two doves flying homeward towards their nest,
with wings raised up and spread and fixed for flight.

And so they came, abandoning the rest
of Dido's group, to glide on the wind's foul gust,
seduced by the sincerity of my request.

"Still-living creature," she said, "so kind and just,
who's traveled through the rank infernal air
to pity us, who've blackened the world with lust.

If we were still God's friends, we'd offer a prayer
that the King of the Universe might mercifully bestow
His peace on you, who've pitied our despair.

And since the whirling winds now cease to blow,
I'll do whatever you wish, and do my best,
and tell you everything you'd like to know.

I was born in a city on the shoreline's eastern crest,
where the waters of the River Po finally depart
and disperse themselves into their ocean's rest.

But Love had captured my Paolo, and right from the start
my sweet soft flesh was all that he was thinking of,
and now that my body's gone, it tears me apart.

Then Love, which exempts no one from the power of love,
offered me Paolo, and I fell under his spell,
and I *still* love him, as I did in the world above.

But Love led to murder, and deep in the depths of Hell,
my husband, who killed us, is, forever, confined."
So I listened to every word she had to tell.

And when she was finished, I fell into a blind
and dark depression and lowered my face,
until Vergil said: "Tell me what's on your mind."

And I said: "What terrible desire to embrace
some sensate love, which seemed both sweet and true,
has led them both to this horrible and hellish place?"

I turned to Francesca: "The pain you're suffering through
rips my sorrowful, weeping heart apart,
and I have nothing but pity for the both of you.

But tell me: When did everything start?
When did Love set your passions free
and reveal the desires hidden within your heart?"

"There's no greater sorrow," she explained to me,
"than remembering happiness while here in pain.
I'm sure that your teacher, Vergil, will agree.

But since you have the desire to ascertain
how everything began, when our passions burned
so out of control, I'll weep as I explain:

One day, for pleasure, we read a book and learned
of Lancelot, how love trapped him within its spell.
At the time, we were alone and unconcerned.

But often, we blushed, as our eyes furtively fell
into each other's, seductively, just before
that terrible moment that brought us here to Hell:

When Lancelot kissed the lips he was longing for,
recklessly throwing his inhibitions away,
then Paolo, who's trapped with me forevermore,

Kissed me on the mouth, and I would have to say
that the book and its pandering author magnified
our lusts, and we read nothing more that day."

While Francesca was speaking, her lover cried,
wailing such a loud and pitiful sound,
I fainted away, as if I'd actually died,

And fell, as a dead body falls to the ground.

Dante Alighieri
(Italian, 1265–1321 C.E.)

Petrarch

Sonnet LXXV

Those beautiful eyes struck out at me
and only those eyes could ease my pain,
not herbs, not sorcery, not some arcane
and magical stone from far across the sea.

Now thoughts of other loves are over and done,
only sweet thoughts of her and her eyes remain,
and if my praises seem wildly unrestrained,
it's Cupid, and not my tongue, that's the guilty one.

Those are the beautiful eyes which always inspire
my lord's victories whenever we're apart.
whenever the war banners fly high in the skies.

Those are the beautiful eyes of my desire
which burn like hidden embers within my heart,
and *never* do I tire of speaking of my lover's eyes!

Francesco Petrarch
(Italian, 1304–1374 C.E.)

Petrarch

Sonnet CCCXII

Not the lovely stars in the cloudless sky,
not the ships adrift on tranquil seas,
not armored knights in the fields nearby,
not happy creatures in the woodland trees.

Not sudden and pleasant news from far away,
not tales of love in soothing poetry,
not chaste and beautiful ladies singing carefree
amid the meadows and fountains on a perfect day.

For nothing can excite this heart which lies
buried in the grave with her, who was to me
the only light that mirrored in my eyes.

Since life is now an endless boring routine,
I call for death, hoping to once again see
the one it would have been best to never have seen.

Francesco Petrarch
(Italian, 1304–1374 C.E.)

Machiavelli

Sonnet

If for a moment, I could stop thinking of you,
I'd call this year the happiest that ever could be.
If I could tell you the pains I'm suffering through,
then I could endure the sorrows torturing me.

If you believed me, I could be content
with the pain your indifferent eyes reflect at me.
Only this forest believes in my misery,
but even the forest is tired of my endless lament.

As for wealth, a son, a kingdom, or a state,
the inevitability of death is well-known,
which is also true of every passion and grief.

But living this life exceeding all pain is my fate!
since you are willing to let me cry alone,
crying without hope, weeping without belief.

> Niccolò di Bernardo dei Machiavelli
> (Italian, 1469–1527 C.E.)

Michelangelo

Dante

It's impossible to properly praise
someone whose splendor burns so bright.
It's easier to curse the ones who didn't treat him right,
than attempt to describe the glory of his ways.

For our instruction, he descended to the catacomb
of hell, then rose to God and went inside,
where the gates of heaven were opened wide,
although he'd been banished from entering his earthly home.

Ungrateful City of Florence! You foolishly cursed
yourself and also destroyed your reputation
by damning him with exile, rejection, and scorn.

Among thousands of other wretched accusations,
the poet's disgraceful exile is the worst,
for a better man than he was never born.

> Michelangelo di Lodovico Buonarroti Simoni
> (Italian, 1475–1564 C.E.)

Garcilaso

Sonnet V

Your lovely face is written in my soul,
and when I write about you and what you do,
it's like *you're* writing it, like I'm not in control,
so I read it in secret and hide it from you.

This is the way I am and always will be,
and though I can't fathom the essence of you,
and though your many virtues are far above me,
I accept them all on faith knowing they're true.

I was born only to love you, my dear,
my soul has been cut to the measure of what you are,
by the habits of my soul, I love you true.

I owe everything to you, it's perfectly clear.
for you I was born, for you I've had my life so far.
I would die for you. I'm always dying for you.

Garcilaso de la Vega
(Spanish, c.1501–1536 C.E.)

Du Bellay

Sonnet XXXI

from Les Regrets

Happy the man, who at his journey's end,
like Ulysses or Jason of the Golden Fleece,
now older and wiser, returns to his home in Greece
to live out his life with loved ones once again!

When will I finish my journeys and finally see
the chimney smoke above my village town
and my little house and garden, then settle down
in the place that means more than any province to me?

I'd rather live in my old ancestral home
than all the lofty palaces of Rome,
more than marble, I prefer gray slate by far,

more than the Tiber, I prefer the lovely Loire,
give me my home, the Palatine can't compare,
even more than breezes from the sea, I crave sweet Anjou air.

> Joachim du Bellay
> (French, 1522–1560 C.E.)

Du Bellay

Sonnet LXXIX

from Les Regrets

I don't write of love, having loved in vain,
I don't write of beauty, not having a girlfriend,
I don't write of gentleness, since I'm a rough end,
I don't write of pleasure, being in pain:

I don't write of happiness, being so bleak,
I don't write of favors, with the princess away.
I don't write of wealth, being as poor as they say,
I don't write of health, being listless and weak:

I don't write of court, since I'm taking a break,
I don't write of France, since I'm no longer there,
I don't write of honor, finding none when I search:

I don't write of friendship, since everyone's fake,
I don't write of virtue, which seems to be nowhere,
I don't write of knowledge, amid the folk of the church.

                    Joachim du Bellay
                    (French, 1522–1560 C.E.)

Camões

Curse

Wipe away, with death, the day of my birth;
may it be forgotten forever, and never
come back in the sweep of time. And if it ever
returns, eclipse the sun and blacken the earth.
Let all light fade and disappear. Let wild
omens reveal that everything must die.
Let monsters be born. Let blood rain from the sky.
Let every mother not recognize her child.
Let all the stunned and terrified people, with tears
streaking down their faces, pale and worn,
believe their world is doomed and overthrown.
You, frightened people, accept these wonders and fears,
for this was the wretched day on which was born
the most miserable life that ever was known.

Luís de Camões
(Portuguese, 1524–1580 C.E.)

Camões

Shipwreck

Like a weary sailor, a refugee
from wreck and storm, who escapes half-dead,
and then, in terror, shudders with dread
at the very mention of the name of the "sea";
who swears he'll never sail again, who raves
he'll stay at home, even on the calmest days,
but then, in time, forgets his fearful ways,
and seeks, again, his fortune above the waves;
I, too, have barely escaped the storms that revolve
around you, my love, traveling far away,
vowing to avoid another catastrophe,
but I can't, the thought of you breaks my resolve,
and so, I return to where, on that fateful day,
I nearly drowned in your tempestuous sea.

Luís de Camões
(Portuguese, 1524–1580 C.E.)

Camões

Dear Gentle Soul

Dear gentle soul, who has, too soon, departed
this life, so discontent: please rest, my dear,
forever in heaven, while I, remaining here,
must live alone, in pain, and broken-hearted.
Within your ethereal state, so high above,
if you are allowed to recall your life below,
remember what you saw, not long ago,
within my eyes, my perfect ardent love.
And if my pain has earned me some relief,
some dispensation, I wonder if you might
in prayer, ask God, who took away your brief
young life, if He would soon, this very night,
give me death, and end my helpless grief,
as swiftly as he took you from my sight.

Luís de Camões
(Portuguese, 1524–1580 C.E.)

Camões

Tagus

Gentle waters of the Tagus, you flow
across the fields, nourishing the herds,
the blooming plants, the flowers, and the birds,
delighting the nymphs and shepherds as you go.
Sweet waters of the Tagus, I don't know when
I'll ever be able to come back home to you,
and, anxiously, before I say adieu,
I begin to doubt if I'll ever return again.
Destiny, intent on finding a way
to turn my joys to sorrows, now commands
this difficult parting, full of regrets and fears.
Still longing for you, and complaining, I sail away,
to breathe my sighs in the airs of foreign lands,
disturbing distant waters with my tears.

Luís de Camões
(Portuguese, 1524–1580 C.E.)

Camões

Natércia

The flaming sun rises high, to the peak
of its ascent in the sky. The goat herds shrink
away from their sweltering fields to drink
the cool refreshing waters from the creek.
The birds, burning in the scorching glare,
find shelter beneath the leaves, within the shade,
and, yet, their lovely songs begin to fade,
and only the humming cicadas fill the air.
Liso is searching for his nymph, although
he always fails, no matter how he tries,
and with a thousand sighs, bemoans his lot.
"Why have you left the one who loves you so,
for one who loves you not?" young Liso cries,
as Echo answers softly, " . . . loves you not."

Luís de Camões
(Portuguese, 1524–1580 C.E.)

Camões

Escape

How strange is life that she should choose to shun
the world, to run away from its deceit,
to hide her youth and beauty, to retreat
beneath the cloak of a Franciscan nun!
But nothing can conceal her grace, mystique,
and marvelous eyes, nothing on earth can hide
her beauty which leaves me totally mystified,
without resistance, helpless and weak.
Whoever keeps her image in mind,
will never be free from pain and all these misguided
hopes and desires which Reason condemns. Whoever,
like me, has seen this glorious woman will find
himself enslaved, for Love has already decided
that she has conquered my heart forever.

Luís de Camões
(Portuguese, 1524–1580 C.E.)

Camões

Exile

Here in this Babylon, that's festering
forth enough evil for the rest of the earth;
Here where true love is denied its worth,
where lustful Venus pollutes everything.
Here where evil is refined and good is cursed,
and tyranny, not honor, has its way;
Here where the Monarchy, in disarray,
blindly attempts to mislead God, and worse.
Here in this labyrinth, where Royalty,
willingly, chooses to succumb
before the Gates of Greed and Infamy;
Here in this murky chaos and delirium,
I carry out my tragic destiny.
But *never* will I forget you, Jerusalem!

Luís de Camões
(Portuguese, 1524–1580 C.E.)

Camões

Sin

Happy is he whose only problem worth
complaining about is love's audacious schemes,
since they alone can never destroy his dreams
of finding some contentment here on earth.
Happy is he who, far from home, embraces
nothing but his long-lost memories,
because when new problems arise, he sees
them clearly, comprehending the sorrow he faces.
And happy is he who lives in *any* state
where only fraud and love's deceits and doubt,
are able to torture his heart from within.
But tragic is he who lives beneath the weight
of some unforgivable act, who lives without
full consciousness of the damages of his sin.

> Luís de Camões
> (Portuguese, 1524–1580 C.E.)

Camões

Nature

The beauty of the sweet, fresh mountains here,
the shade of the green chestnut trees, the pace
of all the gently crawling streams, this place
where all one's sadness seems to disappear.
The hoarse soundings of the sea, the lands that lie
below, the sun hiding near the hills, the last
of the lingering cattle slowly moving past,
the clouds still gently warring in the sky.
But, finally, all these beauties of nature, pouring
forth their various splendors, only create
harsh fresh wounds since you're not here with me.
Without you, everything is disgusting and boring,
without you, I feel, even within this great
natural happiness, the greatest possible misery.

Luís de Camões
(Portuguese, 1524–1580 C.E.)

Camões

Refuge

You who seek serenity in the wide
tempestuous sea of the world, cease
and abandon all hope of ever finding peace,
except in Jesus Christ, God Crucified.
If wealth absorbs your thoughts and preoccupies
your nights, God is the greatest treasure of all;
If you're looking for beauty, always recall
that God alone is the Beauty that satisfies.
If you seek delights to set your heart on fire,
remember that God's the sweetest of all, Who rewards
His followers with victory at last;
If honor and glory are what you most desire,
no greater honor or glory has ever surpassed
humbly serving the highest Lord of Lords.

Luís de Camões
(Portuguese, 1524–1580 C.E.)

Camões

Drowned Lover

Dearest enemy, so often unkind,
my life was in your hands, until that wave
of the sea deprived you of an earthly grave,
depriving me, as well, of peace of mind.
The selfish drowning waters keep us apart,
enjoying your lovely beauty within the vast
cold sea, but as long as my broken life will last,
you'll always be alive within my heart.
And if my ragged poems can last for long
enough, your love, so spotless, will persist
forever and ever, as I, on your behalf,
will praise you always with my singing song;
as long as human memories exist,
my poems will be your missing epitaph.

> Luís de Camões
> (Portuguese, 1524–1580 C.E.)

Camões

Reader

As long as Fortune dangled in my sight
the hope of happiness, my wishful schemes
for lasting love and all my youthful dreams
compelled me to lift my pen and write.
But Love, afraid I might prove indiscreet
and reveal her unpleasant truth, ingeniously
obscured my mind and cruelly tormented me,
trying to keep my pen from exposing her deceit.
But *you*, whom Love has also subjugated
to her fickle will, if you should come across
my verses, this little book of diverse
songs, conceived in experience, created
in truth, remember: the more you've loved and lost,
the better you'll comprehend my verse.

                    Luís de Camões
                    (Portuguese, 1524–1580 C.E.)

Ronsard

Sonnet LIX

Like a deer, when spring is melting the frost away,
who emerges from the woods to eagerly run
beneath the warmth of the rising sun
and graze the honeyed grass at break of day.

Alone, and confident, and carefree,
far from hunters and their dogs, he makes his way
over the hills and valleys throughout the day,
roaming free wherever he'd like to be.

Unafraid of the hunter's net or the archer's bow
until, from nowhere, a sudden lethal blow
is bloodily struck with an arrow's deadly dart.

Thus did I also wander beneath the skies
one carefree April day, when suddenly her eyes
unleashed a thousand arrows into my heart.

Pierre de Ronsard
(French, 1524–1585 C.E.)

Ronsard

Sonnet for Hélène

When you are old and weary late at night,
sitting by the fire, you'll remember Ronsard's rhyme
and sing his verses in the firelight,
recalling that you were beautiful in your time.

And if your servant falls asleep that night,
she'll hear my words, shake off her sleepy ways,
and startle herself awake in the firelight
and bless your name with everlasting praise.

But I'll be a ghost, consigned to death's domain,
lying alone in a darkened myrtle shade.
And you'll be a stooping woman, old and afraid,

regretting my rejected love and your dismissive disdain.
Trust me, *Hélène*, just *live* and don't delay,
and gather the roses of life today.

> Pierre de Ronsard
> (French, 1524–1585 C.E.)

Labé

Sonnet XX

It was once foretold that my future was set,
that I'd fall in love irrevocably
with a lover whose face was described to me,
and, yes, I knew it was him when we first met.

And seeing that he loved me so fervently,
with sorrow, with desperation, I tried to be kind,
and in spite of myself, I made up my mind
to love this lover as much as he loved me.

But who would believe that what the Fates unveil,
what heaven approves, would somehow fail?
I look upward at the darkening sky,

and see the winds and storms swirling above,
convinced that Hades has doomed our love to die
within the tempest of a shipwrecked love.

Louise Charlin Perrin Labé
(French, c.1524–1566 C.E.)

Labé

Sonnet XXIV

Don't reproach me, ladies, and watch what you say,
for I've been suffering a thousand agonies,
and been tortured by a thousand miseries,
crying every single night and day.

So be careful, ladies, of what you say,
since I'm still suffering this catastrophe,
so please don't make things any worse for me.
Besides, what if you're struck in a similar way?

Then don't blame Vulcan for your erotic fires,
and don't blame Adonis's beauty for your desires.
If Cupid wants, he'll compel you to love helplessly,

with far less reason than the one I had,
and make you burn with a wild passion gone mad.
Then try to refrain from being as sad as me!

Louise Charlin Perrin Labé
(French, c.1524–1566 C.E.)

Herrera

For the Battle of Lepanto

From beneath the fearful waves that churn and roar,
great Pontus stir your troubled soul and rise,
and with your dreadful face and hollow eyes
look upon your seas all bloodied with gore.
See the fleets engaged not far from shore,
the Christian west against the Ottoman empire
who furiously battle in smoke and thunder and fire
until the Saracens can fight no more.
And with your deep and powerful voice proclaim
the greatest victory under the watchful sky,
the greatest triumph a man has ever attained.
Then say who all alone has merited such fame,
whose glory on the seas will never die:
the Austrian youth* and the might of Spain.

* John of Austria

Fernando de Herrera
(Spanish, c.1534–1597 C.E.)

Tasso

Vasco

Vasco*, your daring happy sailing ships
set out to face the ever-rising sun,
which lit your days on those courageous trips
until it sank in the sea when day was done.

Your fearless journeys on bitter nights and days,
even more than he who stabbed the Cyclops's eye,
or he who drove the Harpies into the sky,
are much more deserving of lyric praise.

For it was brilliant Camões who made your name
so famous far beyond all the places
you'd traveled when your voyages were finally done.

Now everyone knows of your glorious fame
from the northern pole to distant southern spaces,
for he's made you famous everywhere under the sun.

* Vasco da Gama

Torquato Tasso
(Italian, 1544–1595 C.E.)

De Vega

Sonnet I

from Rimas Sacras

When I pause to contemplate my state
considering the missteps of my days,
I'm astonished that a man so lost in fate
could finally see the error of his ways.

As I look back at my life, I have to admit
that divinely guided reason was abandoned by me,
and only the mercies of heaven kept me free
from falling completely into the evil pit.

I wandered through a labyrinth hoping to find
a way that the feeble thread of my life as it passed
would allow me to see the truth beyond my confusion.

Finally, Your Light expelled the dark from my mind,
and killed the monster of my self-delusion,
so reason, once lost, could now come home at last.

> Lope de Vega
> (Spanish, 1562–1635 C.E.)

De Vega

The Triumph of Judith

Hanging bloody from the bed there lies
the headless shoulders of the inhumane
Holofernes who sieged Bethulia in vain
and brought down angry lightning from the skies.

Beyond his tent's red veil can be seen
the place where the tyrant paid the price:
the hideous barbaric deadly scene,
the decapitated body cold as ice.

His pointless wine-stained armor lying alone,
his table and wine glasses overthrown,
his useless guards asleep at his bloodstained bed.

While high atop the walls of Bethulia that night,
above her people, the beautiful Israelite,
resplendent, holds aloft his severed head.

> Lope de Vega
> (Spanish, 1562–1635 C.E.)

Sor Juana

To Her Portrait

What you see here is a colorful deception.
It's Art creating beauty and mystery
with a falsely-colored sophistry
to subtly deceive your visual perception.

It's an artistic flattery that discreetly
ignores all of life's horrors and fears
and the ravage of time throughout the years,
ignoring old age and oblivion completely.

It's an artifice of vanity and pride,
it's a tender flower tossed in the wind outside,
it's a useless refuge for what is fated to be,

it's a foolish misguided pertinacity,
it's wasted zeal. And when considered overall,
it's corpse, it's dust, it's shadow, it's nothing at all.

Sor Juana Inés de la Cruz
(Spanish, 1648–1695 C.E.)

Bocage

Camões

Camões, how similar, great master,
I find your fate to mine. We both once found
ourselves sailing away from the Tagus bound
for the East to face the sea-god Adamastor.

Like you, at the murmuring Ganges, I sit in a mire
of terrible destitutions and endless terrors;
Like you, with your foolish pleasures and lusty errors,
I'm also the wistful lover of useless desire.

Scornful, like you, of all my bad luck, I grow
despondent, praying for certainty that might create
some peace in the grave whenever my life is through.

You've been my mentor, but sadly, even though
I've imitated you in the sensualities of fate,
I've never, in the arts, been able to emulate you.

Manuel Maria Barbosa du Bocage
(Portuguese, 1765–1805 C.E.)

Bocage

Inês de Castro

The sad and beautiful Inês*, recalling that day,
cries out her tearful echo, which, always repeating,
begs the merciful heavens for justice, entreating
against the assassins who stole her life away.
Her cries are heard at the Fountain of Love in the hours
when the lovely water-nymphs grieve and pray,
where the Mondego, recalling that infamous day,
angrily floods its banks and drowns its flowers.
The universe, itself, offers hymns above
for Pedro, the Prince, who learns of her death then races
to his love, who lies in her grave, to exhume
that miracle of beauty, kindness, and love.
Who opens, beholds, kneels, groans, and embraces;
then crowns his ill-fated Inês within her tomb.

* murdered January 7, 1355

Manuel Maria Barbosa du Bocage
(Portuguese, 1765–1805 C.E.)

Bocage

Self-Portrait

Thin, darkly-complected, and medium-tall,
solid on my feet, with eyes of blue,
sad-faced, with a saddish appearance too,
and a nose that's uppity and not-too-small.

Unable to stay in one place, inclined to aggressions,
rage, unkindness, often lifting up
with innocent hands the darkest cup
and drinking the venom of my lethal hellish obsessions.

The worshipper of a thousand gods. (I've lied:
a thousand girls.) Loving them even before
the sacred altars where the friars pray.

Such is Bocage, in whom some talents reside,
who was struck with all these truths and more,
while he was lounging around one day.

Manuel Maria Barbosa du Bocage
(Portuguese, 1765–1805 C.E.)

Leopardi

Infinity

I've always loved this solitary hill
and even the hedges that partially obscure
the far and distant horizon from my view.
But sitting here and staring off I conjure
the infinite spaces beyond the far horizon,
the inhuman silence, the frightening stillness,
and my heart is almost overcome with fear.
Then I hear winds rustling through the trees
and compare the infinite silences of space
to the voice of the wind, and think of the eternal:
the now-dead seasons of the past,
and the living present with its own sound,
and all these immensities drown my thoughts,
but still it's sweet to shipwreck in such a sea.

Count Giacomo Leopardi
(Italian, 1798–1837 C.E.)

Nerval

Epitaph

Sometimes like a starling he'd happily sing.
Sometimes as a lover, he was tender and kind,
or like Clitandre, of a dark and gloomy mind.
Then one day he heard his doorbell ring.

The visitor was Death! The poet begged and said,
"Please let me finish this sonnet before I go,"
and then, unmoved, he lay himself below
into the freezing coffin, shivered, and was dead.

In life, he was lazy, as the record will show,
his ink dried up, his output was shamefully low.
He craved all knowledge, but ended up stupid and dumb.

Finally, weary of life, it was time to leave,
as his soul was snatched away one winter eve,
as he said as he went, "Why did I bother to come?"

Gérard de Nerval
(French, 1808–1855 C.E.)

Baudelaire

The Albatross

Often, for amusement, crews on their sailing trips
will snare an albatross from the ocean breeze,
one of those huge great birds that follow their ships
as they glide across the bitter depths of the seas.

But down on the deck these displaced kings
seem awkward, ashamed, and undignified,
and even their once-majestic white wings
like useless oars, trail painfully at their side.

How ugly it seems, how laughable and weak,
which once had seemed so beautiful when soaring on high.
A sailor takes his pipe and teases its beak.
Another drags his foot to mock the king of the sky.

The poet shares the fate of this king of the clouds,
who once had ridden the storms, scorning the archer's bow,
but with its giant wings, amid the mocking crowds,
the bird can barely walk on the deck below.

Charles Pierre Baudelaire
(French, 1821–1867 C.E.)

Baudelaire

The Cracked Bell

It's bittersweet on a foggy winter night
to sit beside the fire's crackling log
as memories of the past slowly take flight
at the chiming bells that ring out through the fog.

Happy is the bell that rings so strong,
and which, despite its age, rings confident,
which faithfully chimes out its pious song
like an old soldier keeping watch from his tent.

As for me, my soul is cracked, and in despair,
it tries to fill with song the nighttime air,
but sounds instead like the rattle of death

in a wounded soldier's last and final breath,
who lies beneath a pile of the dead, who lies
abandoned in a pool of blood, then dies.

Charles Pierre Baudelaire
(French, 1821–1867 C.E.)

Baudelaire

To a Woman Passing By

The deafening street was roaring all around me,
as a woman passed, in mourning, in majestic distress,
in sorrow, so tall and slender, and I could see,
when she lifted with her hand, beneath the hem of her dress.

So graceful. I drank her in, as if insane:
the lovely legs, the eyes like the sky when it fills
with a forming tempest, a hurricane,
with softness that fascinates, a pleasure that kills.

Like lightning, then darkness! Her beauty so sublime,
I felt reborn with a fleeting glance. But when
will I ever see her again? The end of time?

So distant! So far! But maybe never again!
We don't even know where the other's going to,
O woman, whom I could have loved. O woman, who knew!

Charles Pierre Baudelaire
(French, 1821–1867 C.E.)

Verlaine

My Recurring Dream

Often I have these strange penetrating dreams
of an unknown woman I love and who loves me,
and every time she comes again I see
she's somehow different, yet still in love it seems.

Who understands me, who understands the fears
within my heart, my fevers, and my despair,
who alone knows how to take such gentle care
while comforting my fevers with her cooling tears.

Was she blonde, brunette, auburn? I'm never sure.
Her name, I remember, was soft, melodious, pure,
like the names of lovers whom life has sent away.

An inert statue, the looks and stares she gave
were lifeless, and her voice was distant, somber, and gray,
with all the inflection of those who lie in the grave.

Paul-Marie Verlaine
(French, 1844–1896 C.E.)

Verlaine

Last Hope

There's a tree that grows in the graveyard alone,
not planted in memoriam for those who have died,
which strives for freedom reaching far and wide,
floating above a simple humble stone.

In both summer and winter upon this tree,
a little songbird comes along
and sings its sad and faithful song.
That little bird is you, that tree is me.

You're the memories, I'm the absence of you,
as recorded by Time as it passes on through . . . .
Ah, to live again! To embrace your knees!

Ah, to live again! But now we're apart
and nothingness has overtaken me, so please,
my dear, assure me that I still live in your heart?

> Paul-Marie Verlaine
> (French, 1844–1896 C.E.)

Corbière

The Toad

A song is heard in the airless night,
the moon's a plate of metallic light
creating spaces of gloomy green.

A song like an echo, alive but weak,
is buried beneath the mountain peak,
lurking but silent in shadows unseen.

A toad! Why does he seem so terrible?
Dear loyal friend, come stand with me
above that wingless poet and see
the Nightingale of the Mud! How horrible!

He sings! Horror! Why do you feel that way?
there's light in his eyes, don't you see?
then beneath a cold rock he slips away.

Bonsoir! That toad down there is me!

Tristan Corbière
(French, 1845–1875 C.E.)

Unamuno

Portugal

At the farthest edge of the Atlantic shore,
a barefoot and disheveled lady peers
into the waves, at the foot of the mountains, and hears
the distant, weeping pines. She sits before
the swirling sea, propping her head in her hands,
and like a lioness, fixes her gazing eyes
on the gateway of the sun, while the ocean cries
its tragic songs of wonders and distant lands.
It sings of tragedies and fate, while she,
with her feet in the foaming surf, dreams of history –
dreams of that once-great empire doomed to be,
so suddenly, lost and drowned in the gloomy sea –
then stares, through the mist, as the King of mystery,
Dom Sebastian, rises from the sea.

Miguel de Unamuno y Jugo
(Spanish, 1864–1936 C.E.)

Valéry

The Lost Wine

One day at a place beside the ocean shore
(I can't remember where it might be)
in tribute to its nothingness I poured
a red and precious wine into the sea.

Who willed it, O wine, and why did I obey?
Perhaps it was an impulse from the divine,
perhaps it surfaced from my heart as a way
of shedding blood while pouring out the wine?

Within the ocean's clear transparency,
the wine's red color of smoky rose
vanished as the sea reclaimed its purity.

But even though the wine was no longer there,
the waves were drunk! And from the seas arose
strange figures that leaped within the bitter air . . .

Ambroise Paul Toussaint Jules Valéry
(French, 1871–1945 C.E.)

Machado

Sonnet II

from "Los sueños dialogados"

Why does my heart fly from where I stand
on the shore of this farming and seafaring land,
where I long for that high Castilian plain
and the rocky wastelands of northern Spain?

Well, no one chooses what they love, so my heart flees
into the gray and barren spaces of long ago,
where the falling mountain northern snow
obliterates the shadows of dead oak trees.

Thinking of Castile I come again
to where the Guadalquivir waters flow,
to offer rosemary sprigs as a gift from me,

for my heart still lies where it was born back then,
born not to life, but born to love, at the Douro Río
at a white-stuccoed wall beneath a cypress tree.

Antonio Machado
(Spanish, 1875–1939 C.E.)

Machado

The Death of the Wounded Child

The hammer of the fever continues to rack
the bandaged temples of the child tonight.
"Mother! See the bird so yellow and bright
and butterflies colored purple and black!"
Squeezing his little hand, his mother laments:
"My flower of fire, how could you possibly freeze?
O flower of my blood, tell me, please?"
Inside, an indigent room with lavender scents,
outside, a round full moon is shedding white light
over the domes and towers of the city at night,
as an airplane drones through the distant sky.
"You're the flower of my blood!" the child is told,
as the windows shudder as the wind whips by.
O, cold, cold, cold, cold, cold!

Antonio Machado
(Spanish, 1875–1939 C.E.)

Angelini

September

September, the air is full of mint tonight
and of the rising moon, and far away
in darkening fields, the flocks appear to sway
gently within the pure enchanted light.

Sometimes, throughout the evening, I can see
the pious farmers working in the field,
like an ancient tale, transfigured and revealed,
like a scene from a Biblical memory.

Within the shifting evening lights, I feel
there lies a hint of autumn whose colors reveal
a message about a judgment that's coming soon.

I also perceive that my own life is winding toward
my final days, as beneath this mystic moon,
I begin my journey back to You, O Lord.

Fra Cesare Angelini
(Italian, 1886–1976 C.E.)

Angelini

December

December, the month of that most holy day,
which makes Christian even the falling snow.
(In whisper, the winds tell everything they know
to the forest and the pebbles in the river-spray.)

And every soul, at this great story, awakens afresh,
reviving their childhoods from ages gone by.
(The country churches speak out and testify,
and all the earth is one great festive crèche.)

So is it snowing again in the countryside?
Where homes, in vigil, comfort and console,
where words, now full of depth, are intensified.

Jesus, tonight, will come again and stay
with the beggar, the finch, and the wandering soul,
who, like a leaf, flutters along the way.

Fra Cesare Angelini
(Italian, 1886–1976 C.E.)

Pessoa

Autopyschography

The poet is a faker,
whose faking is so real,
he even fakes the pain
he actually can feel.

And those who read his poems
don't feel his pain but feel
a pain they really don't have,
that's not exactly real.

While whizzing around the track,
amusing our minds with art,
there circles the wind-up train
we call the human heart.

Fernando António Nogueira Pessoa
(Portuguese, 1888–1935 C.E.)

Pessoa

The Portuguese Sea

O salty sea, how much of your salt
comes from the salty tears of Portugal?
Because of you, how many mothers have cried?
How many loving sons have prayed in vain?
How many brides-to-be have been left alone?
So that, O sea, we could make you our own!

Was it worth it? Of course, it was.
Everything's worth it when the soul is daring.
If you plan to sail beyond Cape Bojador,
you'll need to endure the pains and tragedy.
God made his sea a dangerous abyss,
yet allowed it to mirror heaven upon the sea.

Fernando António Nogueira Pessoa
(Portuguese, 1888–1935 C.E.)

Pessoa

The Child Who Laughs in the Street

The child who laughs in the street,
the song overheard by chance,
the absurdist canvas, the naked statue,
the kindness that has no limit –

All of which exceeds the logic
that reason forces on everything,
and then there's something called love,
even when love is silent.

> Fernando António Nogueira Pessoa
> (Portuguese, 1888–1935 C.E.)

Pessoa

Phantasm

Suddenly, I awake with a terrible fright,
a phantasm's hand emerges from the folds of my sleep
to jar me awake and fearful within the deep
of the dark, unable to sense its shape in the night.

Then an ancient unburied horror overtakes me,
into my heart, as if claiming me for its own,
my lord and master, which descends from its throne
without a nod, a taunt, or royal decree.

And now, I know, my life is suddenly bound,
unconsciously, to this controlling, profound
nocturnal thing. To which I acquiesce,

sensing that I'm nothing, without hope of escape,
the useless shadow of a frightening shape,
existing like the frigid dark in nothingness.

Fernando António Nogueira Pessoa
(Portuguese, 1888–1935 C.E.)

Pessoa

Abdication

Take me in your arms, eternal night,
and call me your son. I'm a king who's ready to disown,
most voluntarily, my royal throne
of weariness and futile dreams tonight.

I give away my sword because it ceases
to be anything but an unwanted burden. Resigned,
I leave my crown and royal scepter behind
inside the antechamber, smashed to pieces.

Next I cast off my worthless coat of mail
and my jingling spurs, so uselessly frail,
leaving them on the frigid palace stairway.

Body and soul, I renounce my sovereign right,
and finally submit to the ancient night,
like a graying countryside at death of day.

Fernando António Nogueira Pessoa
(Portuguese, 1888–1935 C.E.)

Montale

Bring Me the Sunflower

Bring me the flower to plant nearby
in salt-burned soil within this place
to expose all day to the blue-mirrored sky
the anxieties of its yellow face.

Dark things crave the clarity of day,
as bodies vanish in color before long,
as colors vanish in music and song,
for the fate of fate is to fade away.

So bring me the flower that arises
where blond transparencies take flight
where life as essence vaporizes;
Yes, bring me the flower mad with light.

Eugenio Montale
(Italian, 1896–1981 C.E.)

Montale

Pool

Passing over the quivering surface of glass
is the laughter of the belladonna flower,
and pressing through the branches at this hour
the soft and fading clouds slowly pass
reflected on the surface down below.
Then one of us tosses a tiny stone that batters
the bright and shining glass with a sudden blow
and the cloudy apparition shatters.

But look, there's something else in the fading light.
It's slithering across the recomposed glass right now.
It lacks the strength to survive, it can't remain,
it wants to live, but it doesn't know how,
and you watch it slowly sink and fade from sight:
it was born, it died, and it had no name.

Eugenio Montale
(Italian, 1896–1981 C.E.)

Lorca

To Mercedes in Flight

You've* now become a viola of frozen light
which from the highest peaks begins to sing.
A voice without a throat and dark as night,
that sounds through everything, yet not through anything.

Your thoughts are like the snows which shift and turn
in the endless glory of the whiteness above.
Your profile is like an everlasting burn.
Your heart is as free as an untethered dove.

And now, with the endless breeze, sing along
a melody, a fragrant morning song,
like a wounded lily or a mountain of light.

As we, in our corner of sorrow, without relief,
weave for you all day and all of the night,
a garland wreath of melancholy and grief.

* the Count of Yebes's young
daughter who died in 1936

Federico García Lorca
(Spanish, 1898–1936 C.E.)

Lorca

Cottage of the Weeping

I've closed off my balcony
since I don't wish to hear the weeping
yet behind the grayish walls
you can hear nothing but weeping.

There are very few angels singing,
there are very few dogs barking,
a thousand violins fit in the palm of my hand.

But the weeping's an enormous dog,
the weeping's an enormous angel,
the weeping's an enormous violin,
and its tears have muzzled the wind,
and nothing is heard but weeping.

Federico García Lorca
(Spanish, 1898–1936 C.E.)

Borges

Caesar

Here's what the daggers have left on the ground,
this poor pathetic thing, a man who's bled
to death, whose name was "Caesar." The blades have found
their mark, slashing the flesh of the one-now-dead.
So here he lies, after their atrocious crime,
a dead machine used, yesterday, to live
for fame, to execute the history of his time,
enjoying everything his life could give.
But here's *another*, an emperor so discrete
and prudent that once he felt it best
to decline the crown, while commanding the Roman fleet
and an army that conquered both East and West.
Here's also *another* – the one to come – who's hurled
his awesome shadow across the world.

> Jorge Luis Borges
> (Spanish, 1899–1986 C.E.)

Borges

On His Blindness

To the end of my years, I'm wrapped in a shining mist,
a stubborn haze that always hovers near
and reduces all things down to one: to co-exist
without color or form. Almost, to an idea.
The vast elemental night and day,
so full of people, seem nothing but a haze
of light, uncertain yet true, which never fades away,
and lurks in every dawn. I wish I could gaze
upon a face sometime. Or appreciate
these encyclopedias, or other books I hold
in my hands but never can read, or the great
high-soaring birds, or the moons of gold.
For others, there remains the universe,
but in my penumbra, only the habits of verse.

Jorge Luis Borges
(Spanish, 1899–1986 C.E.)

Borges

A Morning in 1649

Charles advances among his people and glances
right and left. Alone, dismissing his well-bred
palace attendants, he calmly walks ahead,
free from self-deception, accepting the circumstances.
He knows he's the king. He knows, not far from here,
he goes to death, though not, he also knows,
into oblivion. The terrible morning grows
more real, his execution waits, but he has no fear.
Like a good gambler, he's always been somewhat
aloof, living his life to the full. Unbowed,
he moves throughout the dangerous crowd.
The chopping block brings no disgrace. His judges are *not*
the ultimate Judge. And then, despite his present trials,
he nods, as he's done so often before, and smiles.

Jorge Luis Borges
(Spanish, 1899–1986 C.E.)

Borges

A Poet of the 13th Century

Once again, he studies the laborious draft
of the very first sonnet, as yet unnamed:
still arbitrary, with its poorly-framed
quatrains and tercets, still lacking the formal craft.
Revising, slowly, he suddenly prevails.
He stops. Something flashes from a future time,
something wondrous, frightening, even sublime,
like the melodious murmur of distant nightingales.
Does he realize that many more sonnets will follow?
That mysterious, incredible Apollo
has revealed a secret, an archetypal thing,
which like a greedy crystal attracts then steals
all that the night conceals and the day reveals:
Daedalus, the maze, the riddle, and Oedipus the King?

Jorge Luis Borges
(Spanish, 1899–1986 C.E.)

Borges

A Soldier of Urbina

Feeling unworthy of yet another campaign,
like his last battle bravely fought at sea,
the soldier* wanders alone in obscurity,
resigned to sordid jobs throughout his native Spain.
To erase, or mitigate, the blackened night
of his reality, he hides within a vast
domain of dreams, within a magical past,
within the cycles of Roland, the Breton knight.
Yet still, he contemplates his deepest pain,
at sunset, observing the copper-colored plain,
convinced he's finished: lonely, impoverished, unknown.
Unaware of the special music which he alone
possesses, where Quixote and Panza and all their schemes
are already stirring alive at the depths of his dreams.

* Cervantes

Jorge Luis Borges
(Spanish, 1899–1986 C.E.)

Borges

Texas

Here too. Here, at the edge of another sea
and continent, there lies another new
and boundless plain where voices vanish and die. Here too:
the Indian, the lasso, and horses running free.
Here too: that secret bird whose sweet song glides
above the roar of historical time, reviving anew
the memory of a forgotten afternoon. Here too:
that mystic alphabet of stars which guides
my pen to scrawl these names from long ago,
still undisturbed within the endless flow
of the labyrinth of time: San Jacinto
and that second Thermopylae, the Alamo.
Here too: that strange, incomprehensible strife,
so brief, so anxious, that we know as life.

Jorge Luis Borges
(Spanish, 1899–1986 C.E.)

Borges

To an Old Poet

In the country fields of Castile, you* walk about,
self-absorbed, aware of nothing and no one.
You reflect on some intricate verse from John, without
a single glance at the yellow, setting sun.
But the shifting dying light, like a ranting fool,
grows delirious, and high above your path
in the east, there expands the scarlet moon of ridicule
and mockery, which just might be the "Mirror of Wrath."
You raise your eyes and stare into the skies,
and a memory of something, something remote,
begins to form but then extinguishes and dies.
Sadly, with your head hung low, you'll soon
continue on your way, having forgotten what you wrote
years ago: *His epitaph is a bloody moon.*

* Quevedo

Jorge Luis Borges
(Spanish, 1899–1986 C.E.)

Borges

The Odyssey, Book Twenty-Three

Already the iron sword of the king has spread
its bloody vengeance. Justice is done.
His arrows and lance have found each and every one
of the insolent suitors who now lie bloodless and dead.
Despite the efforts of a god to undermine
this king, Ulysses has returned to queen and realm,
in spite of storming plots to overwhelm
his ship, in spite of Ares' cries and murderous design.
And now, in the warm love of their bridal bed,
the luminous queen lies sleeping with her head
on the chest of her king. So where's that castaway
who during his exile, night and day, would run
across the world like a wild dog and say
to monsters that his name was "No One"?

Jorge Luis Borges
(Spanish, 1899–1986 C.E.)

Borges

The Borges

I know little or nothing of the Borges,
my ancestors, those Portuguese people lurking here
within my flesh, whose obscure but permanent trace
remains: their habits, their rigor, and their fear.
Shadowy, as if they'd never seen the sun,
these strangers to the processes of art
still form, indecipherably, a part
of time, of earth, and of oblivion.
And justly so, because their labors have prevailed:
they're Portugal – that famous race, at whose command,
the Great Walls of the East were breached, who sailed
out across the seas, to other seas of sand.
They are that fearless king* who vanished inside
the desert, and those, back home, who swear he never died.

* King Sebastian

Jorge Luis Borges
(Spanish, 1899–1986 C.E.)

Borges

To Luís de Camões

Without a shred of pity, time dulls the most
heroic swords, and now, sad Captain, your command
is done, and you've come home to the nostalgic coast
to die within, and with, your native land.
On distant, enchanted, foreign deserts, the flower
of Portugal was lost, unable to endure;
while Spain, no longer subdued and flush with power,
threatens your borders and unprotected shore.
I wonder if you ever understood,
before you crossed that final shore to final rest,
that *everything* which seemed lost and gone for good
– your sword, your flag, the Orient, and the West –
would resurrect, free from the human curse
of change, in *Os Lusíadas*, your epic verse.

Jorge Luis Borges
(Spanish, 1899–1986 C.E.)

Borges

The Sea

Before our dreams (or terrors) persisted
in mythology and cosmogony,
even before time coined itself in days, there existed,
already, the sea. It *was*. There was *always* the sea.
But *who* is the sea? Who is that old, undisciplined,
violent creature, who's gnawing away under
the pillars of the earth, who's also chance and wind,
one and many oceans, abyss and wonder?
Staring upon the sea, we see it as though
for the first time, sensing the splendor of all free
and elemental things: like afternoons, the glow
of the moon, or a blazing fire. But who is the sea?
And who am I? In time, when my days are passed,
and my final agony's done, I'll know, at last.

Jorge Luis Borges
(Spanish, 1899–1986 C.E.)

Borges

Allusion to the Death of Colonel Francisco Borges (1835–1874)

At dusk, I leave him riding on his horse
looking for death. Of all the hours of his past,
this is the image that I'd like to last,
with both its triumph and its bitter remorse.
Solemnly, he moves across the terrain
his white horse and poncho approaching his fate,
while Death, patient in the rifles, lies in wait.
Sadly, Francisco Borges crosses the plain.
This is what surrounds him now: the rifles' roar;
this is what he sees: the endless plains.
This has been his life, it's what remains,
and this has been his place: in battles and war.
So high on his horse in his epic universe,
I leave him as he is, untouched, almost, by my verse.

> Jorge Luis Borges
> (Spanish, 1899–1986 C.E.)

Meireles

Portrait

I didn't always have the face I have today,
so calm, so sad, so thin,
nor these vacant eyes,
nor these bitter lips.

I didn't always have these useless hands,
so cold, so still, so dead,
nor did I have this heart
which never reveals itself.

Nor did I sense the changes when they came,
so simple, so certain, so easy:
In which mirror did I lose
my other face?

Cecília Meireles
(Portuguese, 1901–1964 C.E.)

Meireles

The Rain Rains

The rain falls gently like a silent sleep
that calms and tranquilizes. The rain
rains down with abandon. The rains sweep
down with the musical poetry of Verlaine . . .

which conjures a dream of a gloomy Halloween
and a certain timeless, abandoned palace
which evokes, in the vespers, the lyric and unseen
things of autumn, which poison the soul with malice . . .

Within that distant ancient palace, in that strange
and far-off land, in that misty mountain range,
the organs play moribund arias that murmur along

the huge and ghastly corridors, with winds whipping
beneath the cracks of doors and flipping
the pages of missals, tomes, and books of song . . .

Cecília Meireles
(Portuguese, 1901–1964 C.E.)

Meireles

Joan of Arc

Firm in the saddle of her small panting horse,
she races in the vanguard of her troops as they start
for the enemy trenches, galloping on course,
serene, ecstatic, with a happy heart.

With her hand inside an armored glove,
she holds up high so all can see,
the palpitating flag that flies above
with the golden splendor of the fleur-de-lis.

Confident with dreams, youth, and a faith that's sincere,
the Maid of Orleans in a mystical daze
proceeds undaunted with her missionary aims.

Smile! Not the slightest tremor of fear
invades your soul! But the bold and visionary gaze
already reflects the bonfire's sinister flames.

> Cecília Meireles
> (Portuguese, 1901–1964 C.E.)

Meireles

Spider Hole

Up where even the dust can't reach that high,
she weaves her fragile web, to and fro,
then quickly back and forth, by and by,
without fatigue, mistake, or vertigo.

And when she's done her work, her very best,
she then reveals her magnificent web; then free
at last, the little spider takes her rest,
surrounded by her silken majesty.

The fires of the voluptuous sun ignite
her web, as she sits at its center, a gemstone,
like a glittering tawny topaz, and I believe

this spider is a philosopher, a bright
deserter from the world, all alone,
entangled in the subtle dreams she weaves.

Cecília Meireles
(Portuguese, 1901–1964 C.E.)

Meireles

Herodíada

Mannaeus, panting, returns from the cell of the dead,
carrying in his hands, as he makes his way,
the Baptist's pale and severed head,
dripping with blood on a large and glittering tray.

Which he then offers to Salome,
then Herod, Vitellius, Aulus, and everyone,
who pass it around then silently slip away,
but Phanuel stays after the feast is done.

As the torches' smoky light begins to die,
he stares in terrible silent agony
and clearly sees in John's prophetic eyes:

the meek, who one by one, go passing by,
through wasted landscapes near the Mortuus Sea,
where the placid trickling Jordan lies.

> Cecília Meireles
> (Portuguese, 1901–1964 C.E.)

Meireles

Coimbra Night

Enchanted night! Everything is white,
as though bathed in the pallor of opal. With lulling ease,
the Mondego River seems to fall asleep tonight
and dream beneath the caressing sighs of the breeze.

Tonight, warm with love, everything's at rest,
and yet, the silvery moon wishes it knew
why it's uneasy, why it's distressed,
why it's languid and cold in the faded blue.

In the garden of the sleeping palace, where
the serenading nightingales sing
their love to the flowers, the moon paints everything white,

while, near the fountain, in the sighs of someone there
who's conjured the dead: Pedro, the son of the king,
kisses Inês de Castro in the Coimbra night.

> Cecília Meireles
> (Portuguese, 1901–1964 C.E.)

Andrade

Encounter

My father, lost in time, comes back tonight
through the power of night in this dream of mine.
I sense him instantly as he comes in sight,
and I read his face, line by wrinkled line.

He's dead, so what? Before the dawning day,
I'll watch his face, neither sad nor smiling it seems,
the same old face, and never does he wipe away
a trace of sweat within the calm of my dreams.

Father! Architect and farmer who
built houses of silence and fields of ash,
ever-fertile in the morning dew,

watered by a stream that's always flowing by,
beyond all time, and then, in a sudden flash,
a single breath, our stopped-up springs run dry.

Carlos Drummond de Andrade
(Portuguese, 1902–1987 C.E.)

Brief Biographies:

ANDRADE: Carlos Drummond de Andrade (1902–1987) is considered one of the most significant poets in Brazilian history. He was born to a farming family in Itabira, trained to be a pharmacist, but spent most of his adult life working as a civil servant.

ANGELINI: Cesare Angelini (1886–1976) was born into a peasant family in Albuzzano, Italy. After completing his studies at the seminary in Pavia, he was ordained a Catholic priest. During World War I, he served as an army chaplain, then later as the rector of Almo Collegio Borromeo in Pavia.

ANONYMOUS: *La Chanson de Roland* about Charlemagne's nephew Roland at the Battle of Roncevaux Pass in 778 was probably written somewhere between 1040 and 1115. Although the author is generally considered anonymous, the name "Turoldus" appears at the end of the poem's oldest surviving manuscript at the Bodleian Library at Oxford. *La Chanson de Roland* is the national epic of France.

ANONYMOUS: *El Cantar de mio Cid* is set in the 11th century and narrates stories about the Castilian warrior Rodrigo Díaz de Vivar known as El Cid. The author is unknown, and its composition, certainly influenced by *La Chanson de Roland,* has been estimated between 1140 and 1207. *El Cantar de mio Cid* is the national epic of Spain.

BAUDELAIRE: Charles Pierre Baudelaire (1821–1867) was born in Paris, France. He studied law at the Lycée Louis-le-Grand, but he was more interested in the bohemian lifestyle that alienated him from his family. His influential first volume, *Les Fleurs du mal* (1857), made him both famous and infamous. He was also a distinguished translator and essayist.

BOCAGE: Manuel Maria Barbosa du Bocage (1765–1805) was born in Setúbal, Portugal. A child prodigy, he would lead a contentious and wandering life and was often considered unstable by his contemporaries. After an unsuccessful attempt at a military career, he went to the Orient like his hero Luís de Camões. When he returned to Lisbon, he was arrested and jailed for alleged subversive opinions.

BORGES: Jorge Luis Borges (1899–1986) was one of the most important literary figures of the 20th century. Born in Buenos Aires, Argentina, to a middle-class family, he later studied at the Collège de Genève in Switzerland. He was eventually appointed as the director of the National Public Library in Buenos Aires. He was a master of the sonnet, as well as a master of the short story.

CAMÕES: Luís de Camões (1524–1580), considered the greatest poet in Portuguese history, led an extraordinary life. He was a regular at the royal court, lost an eye fighting the Moors in Morocco, was arrested for stabbing a royal favorite in a street brawl, and was banished to the Eastern Empire. In Asia, he fought in several military campaigns, served as a government official in Macao, was charged with embezzlement, was shipwrecked off Cambodia, was jailed twice in Goa, and was stranded penniless in Mozambique. Eventually, he returned to Lisbon where he died during an outbreak of the plague. His versatile sonnets are among the best in world literature, and he also wrote the last great Western epic, *Os Lusíadas*.

CATULLUS: Gāius Valerius Catullus (c.84–c.54 B.C.E.) was born into a prominent family in Verona. The specific facts of his life are few, but it seems clear that he lived in Rome for a period. His extremely influential poems often focused on personal matters, including numerous love poems to "Lesbia."

CORBIÈRE: Tristan Corbière (1845–1875) was born in Ploujean, France. He studied at the Lycée de Saint-Brieuc and suffered from severe rheumatism and other physical disabilities. He spent most of his short life in Ploujean and published one volume of poetry, *Les Amours Jaunes*.

DANTE: Dante Alighieri (1265–1321) is one of the world's most celebrated poets. Born in Florence, Italy, he fought in the cavalry at the Battle of Campaldino. His involvement in Florentine politics eventually lead to his banishment from the city, and he never returned. He spent his final two years in Ravenna, where he completed the *Divine Comedy*. T.S. Eliot has written that "Dante and Shakespeare divide the world between them."

DE VEGA: Lope de Vega (1562–1635) was born in Madrid, where his father was an embroiderer. After study at the University of Alcalá, he joined the Spanish Navy and was fortunate to survive the defeat of the Armada, returning to Madrid in one of the fleet's few surviving ships. In Madrid, he became both a renowned poet and playwright, and he was ordained a Catholic priest in 1614.

DU BELLAY: Joachim du Bellay (1522–1560) was born at the Castle of La Turmelière near Liré, France. He studied law at the University of Poitiers and became friends with Pierre de Ronsard. They went to Paris together where Du Bellay involved himself in literary circles and literary controversies. Like Ronsard and Labé, he is considered a master of the French sonnet.

GARCILASO: Garcilaso de la Vega (c.1501–1536) was born in Toledo, Spain, to a noble family. Highly educated, he joined the military and served Charles V during numerous campaigns throughout Europe. His poetry was well-known in contemporary literary circles and remained highly influential after his death.

HERRERA: Fernando de Herrera (c.1534–1597) was born in Seville, Spain, to a respected family. Unlike his poetic hero Garcilaso de la Vega, Herrera led a mostly solitary life and eventually took minor orders in the Catholic Church. His poetry was highly influential, and his admirer Cervantes referred to him as "el Divino."

HORACE: Quintus Horatius Flaccus (65–8 B.C.E.) was born in Venusia in southern Italy. He served as an officer in the defeated Republican army at the Battle of Philippi in 42 B.C., but he was eventually befriended by Octavian's confidant, Maecenas, and became associated with the new regime. One of the most distinguished poets of the Roman Empire, he was famous for his versatile odes, satires, epistles, and epodes.

LABÉ: Louise Charlin Perrin Labé (c.1524–1566) was born in Lyon, France, to a wealthy ropemaker. An excellent horsewoman, she was also well-educated, and her poems, particularly her sonnets, were highly regarded both during her lifetime and after her death.

LEOPARDI: Count Giacomo Leopardi (1798–1837) was born into a noble family in Recanati in the Italian Papal States. A prodigy in his youth, he was also sickly and spent many years in his father's extensive library. Although Leopardi spent most of his life in Recanati, he did manage to visit Rome, Florence, and several other cities on the Italian peninsula.

LORCA: Federico García Lorca (1898–1936) was born in Fuente Vaqueros near Granada in southern Spain to a wealthy farming family. He attended the University of Granada before moving to Madrid where he became friends with Luis Buñuel and Salvador Dalí and began writing poems and avant-garde plays. An outspoken socialist, Lorca was arrested and killed by Nationalist militia in 1936.

MACHADO: Antonio Machado (1875–1939) was born in Seville, Spain, and educated at the Institución Libre de Enseñanza in Madrid. After working in Paris as a translator, he returned to Spain, eventually serving as a Professor of French at the Instituto de Segovia. During the Spanish Civil War, he and his elderly mother were evacuated several times, ending up in Collioure, France, where he died in 1939.

MACHIAVELLI: Niccolò di Bernardo dei Machiavelli (1469–1527) was one of the most important political philosophers in world history, especially for his two treatises *The Prince* and *Discourses on Livy*. Born in Florence, he served as an Italian diplomat, and he also wrote poetry and two plays, *Mandragola* and *Clizia*.

MARTIAL: Marcus Valerius Martialis (c.40–c.104) was born in Augusta Bilbilis in Hispania Tarraconensis, a Roman province in modern-day Spain. He eventually moved to Rome and is most famous for his collections of clever epigrams.

MEIRELES: Cecília Meireles (1901–1964) is one of the most renowned poets in Brazilian history. Born in Rio de Janeiro, she spent her life as an educator teaching mostly in public schools. In 1936 she was appointed lecturer at Universidade Federal in Rio de Janeiro.

MICHELANGELO: Michelangelo di Lodovico Buonarroti Simoni (1475–1564), one of the world's most famous artists, was also a serious poet. Although born in Caprese, Tuscany, he was raised in Florence. He is particularly renowned for his sculptures, the *Pietà* and *David*, and for the frescoed ceiling of the Sistine Chapel in the Vatican.

MONTALE: Eugenio Montale (1896–1981) was born in Genoa, Italy, to a business family. Essentially self-taught, he worked as an accountant, then served briefly in World War I as an infantry officer. He later lived in Florence and Milan, receiving the Nobel Prize in 1975.

NERVAL: Gérard de Nerval (1808–1855) was the pen name of Gérard Labrunie. He was born in Paris, the son of an army medic. He studied at Collège Charlemagne and later worked as a notary, a translator, and a journalist. He traveled extensively, but eventually fell into poverty and took his own life in Paris in 1855.

PESSOA: Fernando António Nogueira Pessoa (1888–1935) was the most important Portuguese poet of the 20th century. After spending much of his youth in Durban, South Africa, he returned to Lisbon and was soon involved in its active literary scene. His poetry is unique in its use of various heteronyms, each with its own biographical history and literary style.

PETRARCH: Francesco Petrarca (1304–1374) was one of the most important and influential figures of the Italian Renaissance. He was born in Arezzo, Italy, and studied law at the University of Montpellier and the University of Bologna. He traveled all over Europe, often serving as an ambassador, and died of the plague in Padua in 1374.

RONSARD: Pierre de Ronsard (1524–1585) was born in Couture-sur-Loir, France. He studied at the Collège de Navarre in Paris and after abandoning his diplomatic career, he formed the literary group La Pléiade with Joachim du Bellay and several other poets. He became famous during his lifetime and remains a major influence on French literature.

SOR JUANA: Sor Juana Inés de la Cruz (1648–1695) was born Inés de Asbaje y Ramírez de Santillana in San Miguel Nepantla near Mexico City. The illegitimate daughter of a disengaged Spanish officer, she grew up comfortably on her maternal grandfather's estate. After serving as a lady-in-waiting at the court of the colonial viceroy, she decided to became a Hieronymite nun. Renowned for her erudition and her literary accomplishments, she became famous throughout New Spain.

TASSO: Torquato Tasso (1544–1595), one of the most important literary figures in Italian history, was born into a noble family in Sorrento. A prodigy in his youth, he was already famous by the age of eight. Aside from his numerous sonnets, his other significant works include the epic poem *Gerusalemme Liberata* about the siege of Jerusalem during the First Crusade in 1099. Despite his brilliance, Tasso was also mentally unstable, and he spent seven years in the madhouse at St. Anna's in Ferrara.

UNAMUNO: Miguel de Unamuno y Jugo (1864–1936) was a renowned essayist, novelist, poet, playwright, and philosopher. Born in Bilbao, Spain, he completed his doctorate at the University of Madrid and eventually became a professor of Greek at the University of Salamanca, where he later became rector of the university. A prodigious author, Unamuno was an important intellectual figure in Europe in the early 20th century.

VALÉRY: Ambroise Paul Toussaint Jules Valéry (1871–1945) was born in Sète, France, and studied law at the Collège de France in Paris. While working in government service, he became a member of the literary circle surrounding Stéphane Mallarmé. Despite a late period of literary silence that lasted for twenty years, Valéry was a prodigious author of poetry, essays, and fiction.

VERGIL: Publius Vergilius Maro (70–19 B.C.E.) is generally considered the Roman Empire's greatest poet. He was born in Andes, Cisalpine Gaul, in northern Italy, and he studied in Cremona, Mediolanum, Rome, and Naples. He was the influential author of the *Eclogues,* the *Georgics,* and the *Aeneid,* the national epic of ancient Rome.

VERLAINE: Paul-Marie Verlaine (1844–1896) was born in Metz, France, and educated at the Lycée Impérial Bonaparte. He served briefly in the military and worked as a civil servant. One of the most talented of the Symbolist poets, Verlaine was also considered a "decadent" poet, and his addiction to drugs and alcohol eventually lead to his death in 1896.

About The Translator:

William Baer, a Guggenheim fellow, is the author of forty books including seven collections of poetry, most recently *Formal Salutations: New & Selected Poems*. His various other books include *Luís de Camões: Selected Sonnets*; *"Bocage" and Other Sonnets* (recipient of the X.J. Kennedy Poetry Prize); *Psalter*; *Classic American Films: Conversations with the Screenwriters*; *Writing Metrical Poetry*; and *The Unfortunates* (recipient of the T.S. Eliot Award). A graduate of Rutgers and N.Y.U., he received his doctorate at the University of South Carolina under the direction of James Dickey. He also has graduate degrees from The Writing Seminars at Johns Hopkins and the School of Cinematic Arts at the University of Southern California where he received the Jack Nicholson Screenwriting Award. A former Fulbright (Portugal) and the recipient of a NEA Creative Writing Fellowship, he is also the author of two collections of short fiction (*Times Square and Other Stories* and *One-and-Twenty Tales*) and six novels including the *New Jersey Noir* series, *Advocatus Diaboli*, *Companion*, and *Murder in Times Square*. His various plays have been performed at over thirty American theaters.

Website: williambaer.net